Nelson

English

Beginning
Fiction Skills

**YELLOW
LEVEL**

John Jackman   Wendy Wren

Text © John Jackman and Wendy Wren 2001
Original illustrations © Nelson Thornes Ltd 2001

Published in 2001 by:
Nelson Thornes Ltd
Delta Place
27 Bath Road
CHELTENHAM
GL53 7TH
United Kingdom

06 07 08 / 10 9 8 7 6 5

A catalogue record for this book is available from the British Library

ISBN 0-17-424811-3

Illustrations by Carol Daniels, Sue King, Mary Lonsdale, Gilly Marklew, Terry Riley, Lisa Smith, Liz Sawyer, Mike Walsh, Amanda Wood
Page make-up by Clive Sutherland

Printed and bound in Croatia by Zrinski

The authors and publisher wish to thank the following for permission to use copyright material: A P Watt Ltd on behalf of the author for an extract from Dick King-Smith *The* Hodgeheg; The Ciardi Family for John Ciardi, 'I Wouldn't' from *You Read to Me, I'll Read to you* by John Ciardi, HarperCollins (1962); Charles Thomson for 'Dragon in the Classroom' (1991); HarperCollins Publishers, Inc for Jack Prelutsky, 'I Wonder Why Dad is so Thoroughly Mad' from *The New Kid on the Block* by Jack Prelutsky, copyright © 1984 by Jack Prelutsky; HarperCollins Publishers for an extract and illustrations from Nick Butterworth, *One Snowy Night* (1989).

Every effort has been made to trace copyright holders and to obtain their permission for the use of copyright material. The publishers will gladly receive any information enabling them to rectify any error or omission in subsequent editions.

Contents

Secrets

Jimmy is not good at keeping secrets. He gives away secrets so often that his friends are careful not to tell him any.

The next morning when Jimmy went to school he stopped outside the door. He listened. He heard someone say, "Shhhh! He's outside. He's listening. Don't give it away."

Everything got very quiet. Jimmy walked into the room and sat at his desk. In a low voice he said, "Please tell me the secret, Roman."

"No."

"I'd tell you."

"I know you would."

"Pleasssssssse!"

"Nnnnnoooooooo."

"Then I'll find out from somebody else."

After school he waited at the corner for Libby. In Class One Libby had had trouble keeping a secret too. She had told that Rickie had a little snake in his pocket. Well, she had not actually told. She had said, "Mr Rogers, is it all right for us to bring snakes to school in our pockets?"

When he saw Libby, Jimmy said, "Libby, what's the big secret?"

Libby said, "I'm not telling."

"If I ever hear a secret, I'm not going to tell you."

"You're never going to hear one."

He followed Libby down the sidewalk on his knees. "Please please please please –"

"Oh, all right," Libby said. "Our teacher's going to get married."

He got up and dusted off his knees. He ran home like a cartoon character, leaving a streak behind him. He flung open the door. "I found out the secret! Our teacher's going to get married."

"She's already married," his mother said. "Somebody's teasing you."

Comprehension

1 What did Jimmy want Roman to tell him?

2 Who did Jimmy wait for after school?

3 Who had a little snake in his pocket?

4 What secret did Libby tell Jimmy?

5 What did Jimmy do as soon as he found out the secret?

Spelling

'ing' and 'ed'

Action words are called **verbs**.

Some words, like 'wait', are **action words**. Sometimes we add 'ing' or 'ed' to action words. For example:

wait   wait**ing**   wait**ed**

A Choose an action word from the box to go with each picture.
Write down the word.
Write it again, adding 'ing' and then 'ed'.
The first one has been done to help you.

jump ✓   kick   walk   shout   talk

1   jump
jumping
jumped

2

3

4

5

B 1   Copy each word and add 'ing'.

a speak   b guess   c miss

d listen   e hear   f tell

2   Copy each word and add 'ed'.

a want   b learn   c watch

d pass   e help   f wait

Writing sentences

Capital letters

> **Special naming words** begin with a capital letter.
> For example:
> Jimmy   Libby   Glasgow   Friday

A Copy each sentence and finish it with a special naming word.

1 My first name is _____ .

2 My last name is _____ .

3 The name of my best friend is _____ .

B Copy all the special naming words in the story on pages 4 and 5.

Writing

Writing a story

Look at the pictures below.
They tell the main parts of the story on pages 4 and 5.
They are jumbled up.

A

1 Which picture shows the **beginning** of the story?
Write a sentence about it, starting

When Jimmy got to school, he _____ .

B

2 Which picture shows the **middle** of the story?
Write a sentence about it, starting

After school, he _____ .

C

3 Which picture shows the **end** of the story?
Write a sentence about it, starting

As soon as Jimmy got home, he _____ .

7

The Hodgeheg

Max is a small hedgehog who wants to know how to cross a busy road.

It was the evening rush-hour and the homegoing traffic was at its heaviest. Cars and motor-bikes, buses and lorries thundered past, terrifyingly close it seemed to him, as he crouched outside the gate, and he was confused and dazzled by their lights. The streetlamps too lit up the place like day, and Max, nocturnal by nature, made for the darkest spot he could find, in the shadow of a tall litter-bin, and crouched there with hammering heart.

Gradually he grew a little more accustomed to the din and the glare, and, though he dared not move, began to observe the humans, for numbers of pedestrians passed close by him.

They were all walking on the narrow road on which he sat, a road raised above the level of the street itself by about the height of a hedgehog. "They're safe," said Max to himself, "because the noisy monsters aren't allowed up here."

He looked across the street, and he could see that at the far side of it there were other humans, also walking safely on a similar raised road. He did not however happen to see any cross the street.

"But they must cross somewhere," said Max. "There must be a place further along the street."

Comprehension

Write a short sentence to answer each question.

1   What time of the day was it?

2   Where did Max make for so he would be safe?

3   Why did Max think the humans were safe?

4   What did Max see across the street?

5   What did Max think there must be further along the street?

6   What do you think these words in the story mean?

    a   crouched   b   din   c   narrow

7   The humans were walking on 'a road raised above the level of the street'. What do we call this?

8   What do you think the 'noisy monsters' were?

9

Spelling

'ow' and 'ou'

Sometimes, different groups of letters can make the same sound. The letters '**ow**' sometimes make the same sound as the letters '**ou**'. For example:

An **ow**l watched as Max cr**ou**ched near the kerb.

A Write a word from the box to go with each picture below. The first one has been done to help you.

mouse
owl ✓
house
flower
town
cloud
mouth
towel
shower

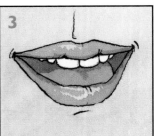
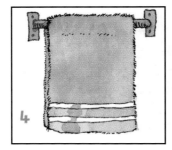

1 owl

B Copy and complete each word by adding 'ow' or 'ou'.

1 cl _ _ n   2 d _ _ n   3 pr _ _ d

4 l _ _ d   5 br _ _ n   6 s _ _ n d

7 sp _ _ t   8 gr _ _ l   9 cr _ _ d

Writing sentences

Capital letters and full stops

A sentence starts with a **capital letter**. A sentence ends with a **full stop**. For example:

The little hedgehog wants to cross the road.

A Copy each letter below.

Then, write each letter as a capital letter.

The first one has been done to help you.

1 a A   2 o ___   3 c ___   4 p ___   5 d ___

B Copy these sentences.

Put in the missing capital letters and full stops.

1 it is hard for animals to cross the road safely

2 many animals are killed on the road

3 they are often dazzled by car lights

Writing

Stories

The hedgehog below has found a safe place to cross the road.
Write about what the hedgehog is doing and what you can see in the picture.
Use words from the box to help you.

zebra crossing   car   crossed   bicycle   hedgehog   cross
lights   stopped   across   walk   stepped   road

I Wouldn't

There's a mouse house
In the hall wall
With a small door
By the hall floor
Where the fat cat
Sits all day,
Sits that way
All day
Every day
Just to say,
"Come out and play"
To the nice mice
In the mouse house
In the hall wall
With the small door
By the hall floor.

And do they
Come out and play
When the fat cat
Asks them to?

Well, would you?

Comprehension

A Answer these questions about the poem.

1 Where is the cat sitting?

2 Where is the small door?

3 Does the cat really want to play with the mice?

4 If you were one of the mice, would you come out? Why?

5 What do you think it is like in the 'mouse house'?

B Copy the words below.
Beside each word, write another word from the poem that rhymes.
The first one has been done to help you.

1 mouse *house*   2 floor

3 nice   4 fat

5 wall   6 say

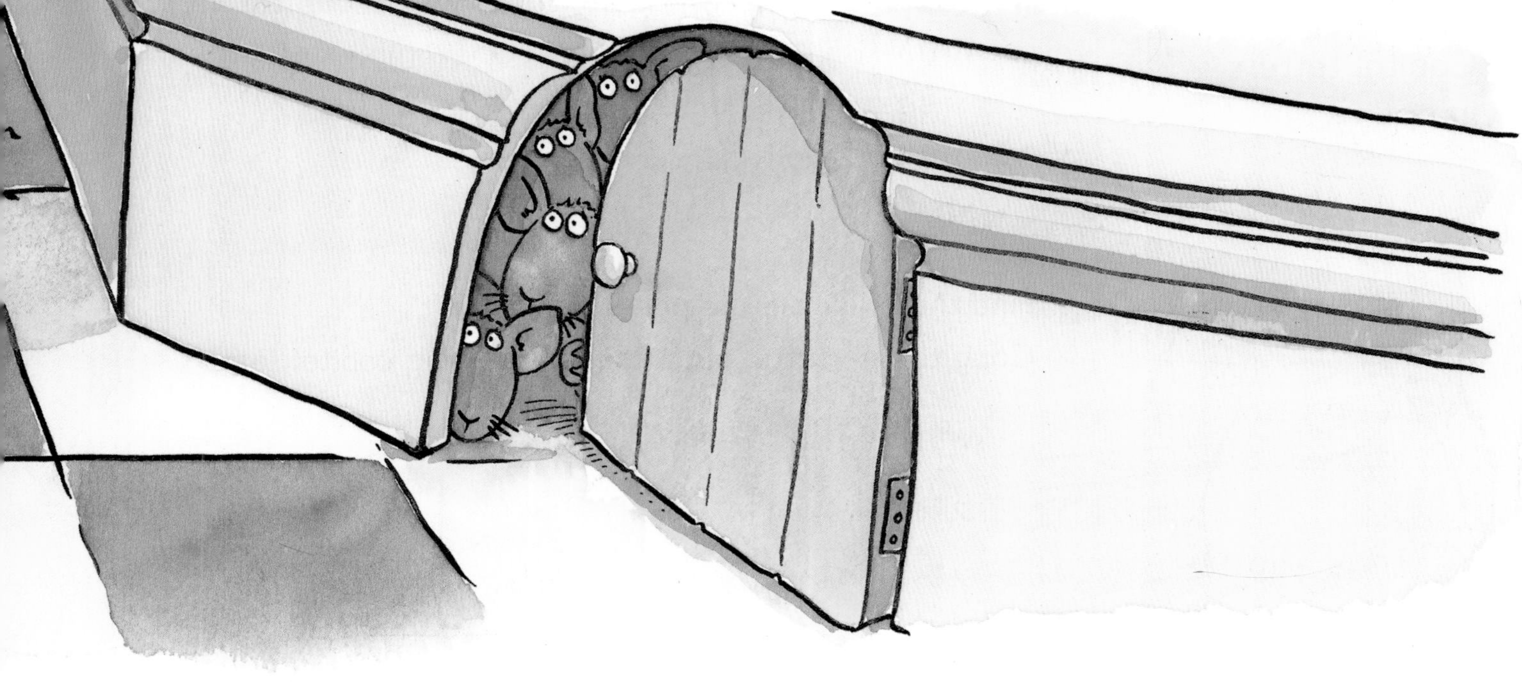

Spelling

'ai', 'ay' and 'a-e'

Sometimes, different groups of letters can make the same sound. The letters '**ai**', '**ay**' and '**a-e**' sometimes sound the same. For example:

Don't be afr**ai**d mice. I only want to pl**ay** a g**a**m**e** with you.

A Choose the correct word to go with each picture.
Write your answers.

1 bay   bale   2 lay   lane   3 ray   rain   4 play   plane

B Copy and complete each word, by adding 'ai', 'ay' or 'a-e'.

1 c__k__   2 h___   3 s___l
4 g__t__   5 br___n   6 r___l
7 str___   8 gr__p__s   9 cl___

Writing sentences

Capital letters
in poems

Each new line of a poem usually starts with a **capital letter**, even when it isn't a new sentence. For example:

There's a mouse house
In the hall wall
With a small door

A Find these lines in the poem 'I wouldn't'.
Copy them neatly, putting in the missing capital letters.

where the fat cat
sits all day,
sits that way
all day

B Neatly copy these lines from a poem about Noah's ark.
Put in the missing capital letters.

the animals went in two by two,

the crocodile and the kangaroo.

the animals went in three by three,

the tall giraffe and the tiny flea.

Writing

Rhymes

'I wouldn't' is a rhyming poem.
Copy the pairs of rhyming lines below.
Use the correct word from the box to fill each gap.

door   mouse   cat   wall

In the hall

There's a _____ .

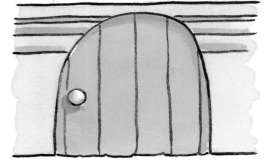

Near the floor

There's a _____ .

In the house

There's a _____ .

On the mat

There's a _____ .

15

Check-up 1

Spelling

A For each picture, choose the correct **action word** from the box. Add **'ing'** or **'ed'** to the action word so that it describes the action in the picture.

| paint   jump   kick   eat |

1

2

3

4

B Write an **'ou'** or **'ow'** word to go with each picture.

1

2

3

4

C Write an **'ai'**, **'ay'** or **'a-e'** word to go with each picture. The first letter of each word has been given.

1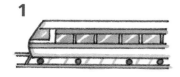

t _____

2

r _____

3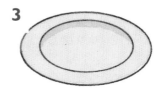

p_____

4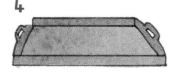

t _____

5

n _____

6

l _____

7

t _____

8

s _____

16

Writing sentences **A** Write each letter as a **capital letter**.

1 y __   2 t __   3 h __   4 k __

5 b __   6 u __   7 e __   8 f __

9 j __   10 m __   11 w __   12 r __

B Copy the words from the box.
Add capital letters to the **special naming words**.

| boy | peter | monday | school | katy | cat |

C Copy these sentences.
Put in the missing **capital letters** and **full stops**.

1 my brother has hurt his leg

2 it rained all day

3 we had pizza for tea

4 soon it will be my birthday

D Copy the lines of poetry below.
Add the missing **capital letters**.

the animals went in four by four,

the hippopotamus stuck in the door.

the animals went in five by five,

the bees mistook the bear for a hive.

Little Red Riding Hood

One day, Little Red Riding Hood's mother called her in from the garden.

"Little Red Riding Hood, will you take this basket of food to your grandmother? She is not very well and I want her to have something good to eat."

"Yes," said Little Red Riding Hood. "I will pick some of the red flowers and take them, too."

Little Red Riding Hood picked the flowers in the bright, sunny garden. She took the basket of food and set off into the wood.

As she walked along the narrow path, it became very dark. There were big trees on either side. They grew very close together and blotted out the sun. A few flowers grew on the edge of the path but they were not big and bright like the flowers in the garden. They were very small and pale.

The path grew narrower. The wood grew darker and colder. As Little Red Riding Hood turned a corner, she saw a dark shape standing in the middle of the path . . .

Comprehension

1   What did Little Red Riding Hood's mother ask her to do?

2   Why did Little Red Riding Hood's mother want her to do that?

3   As well as the basket of food, what did Little Red Riding Hood take with her?

4   How do you think Little Red Riding Hood was feeling when she set off? Why?

5   How do you think Little Red Riding Hood was feeling when she was alone in the wood? Why?

6   How do you think Little Red Riding Hood was feeling when she saw 'a dark shape standing in the middle of the path'? Why?

Spelling

Opposites

Opposites are called **antonyms**.

Some words have **opposites**. For example:

The flowers were small.   The flowers were big.

A Copy each word below and then write another word that means the opposite.
The first one has been done to help you.

1 empty   empty   full

2 up   3 yes   4 under

5 day   6 good   7 happy

8 young   9 dry   10 long

Letters added at the beginning of a word are called a **prefix**.

B 1 Make the opposite of each word by adding either 'un' or 'dis' at the beginning.
The first one has been done to help you.

a tie   untie

b appear   c lucky   d true

e obey   f tidy   g agree

2 Write a sentence using one of the new words you made in question 1.

Writing sentences

'was' and 'were'

We use '**was**' when we are writing about one person or thing. For example:

Grandmother was unwell.

We use '**were**' when we are writing about more than one person or thing. For example:

Red Riding Hood and her mother were worried.

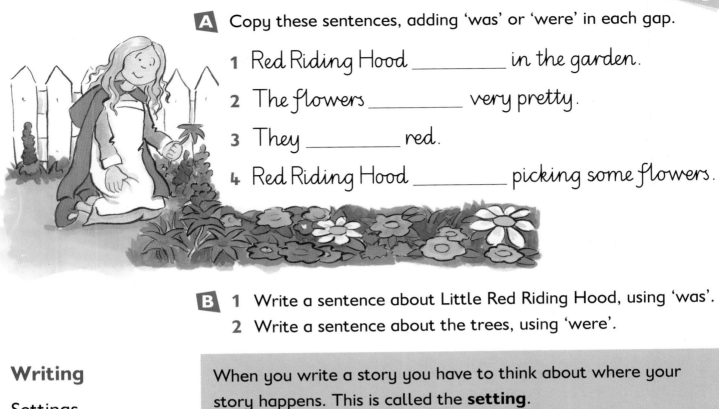

A Copy these sentences, adding 'was' or 'were' in each gap.

1 Red Riding Hood _____ in the garden.

2 The flowers _____ very pretty.

3 They _____ red.

4 Red Riding Hood _____ picking some flowers.

B 1 Write a sentence about Little Red Riding Hood, using 'was'.

2 Write a sentence about the trees, using 'were'.

Writing

Settings

When you write a story you have to think about where your story happens. This is called the **setting**.

The first part of the story of Little Red Riding Hood happens in the garden and the second part happens in the wood.

A 1 Find and copy two words which tell you what it was like in:

   a the garden

   b the wood.

2 Make a list of other words that you could use to say what it was like in:

   a the garden

   b the wood.

B 1 Use your words from part A to write a sentence about the garden, starting

In the garden it was _____

2 Use your words from part A to write a sentence about the wood, starting

In the wood it was _____

A Dragon in the Classroom

There's a dragon in the classroom:
its body is a box,
its head's a plastic waste-bin,
its eyes are broken clocks,

its legs are cardboard tubes,
its claws are toilet rolls,
its tongue's my dad's old tie
(that's why it's full of holes).

'Oh, what a lovely dragon,'
our teacher smiled and said.
'You *are* a pretty dragon,'
she laughed and stroked its head.

'Oh, no I'm not,' he snorted,
SNAP! SNAP! he moved his jaw
and chased our screaming teacher
along the corridor.

Charles Thomson

Comprehension

1 Write the title of the poem.

2 Write the name of the poet.

3 How many verses are in the poem?

4 Make a list of the things the dragon is made from.

5 For each verse, write the pair of words that rhyme.

6 How do you think the dragon came to be in the classroom?

7 What is the surprise in the last verse?

8 Explain why you like or do not like this poem.

Spelling

Syllables

Like music, words have beats.

The beats in words are called **syllables**.

Say these words aloud:

| box | dragon | corridor |

Box   has <u>one</u> syllable.

Dra/gon   has <u>two</u> syllables.

Cor/ri/dor   has <u>three</u> syllables.

A   Read and copy each word below.

Then split each word into its syllables.

The first one has been done to help you.

1 broken   bro/ken   2 cardboard

3 plastic   4 exciting   5 lovely

6 snorted   7 leg   8 wonderful

B   Write three words of your own that each have:
- two syllables
- three syllables.

Writing sentences

Speech bubbles

The words in these **speech bubbles** were said by the teacher and by the dragon.

Teacher   Dragon

A
1 Who said, "Oh, what a lovely dragon."?
2 Who said, "Oh, no I'm not."?

B Draw a picture of the dragon chasing the teacher.
Draw a speech bubble for each of them.
Inside, write what you think they are shouting.

Writing

Dragon poem

Imagine you have made a dragon at school, out of odd bits and pieces.

1 Make a list of things you might have used to make your dragon.

2 Write a poem which describes what your dragon is made of and what it looks like.
Use this line to start your poem:

There's a dragon in the classroom

The Three Billy Goats Gruff

The Three Billy Goats Gruff were very hungry. Middle Billy Goat Gruff had eaten all the grass in the field.

"Let's go across the bridge to that other field," said Little Billy Goat Gruff. "There is plenty of good grass there."

"What about the troll?" said Big Billy Goat Gruff. "If we try to cross the bridge he will eat us for his supper. I don't want to be eaten!"

"We need some more grass to eat," said Middle Billy Goat Gruff. "Little Billy Goat Gruff can go first."

Little Billy Goat Gruff did not want to cross the bridge first but he always did as he was told. He went trip-trap, trip-trap over the bridge. The horrible, terrible troll heard Little Billy Goat Gruff and jumped out with a loud roar.

"Who is crossing my bridge?" he cried. "I will eat you for my supper!"

Middle Billy Goat Gruff shouted to Little Billy Goat Gruff, "Go on! Go on! We must have some grass to eat."

Big Billy Goat Gruff ran and hid behind a tree. "The troll will eat Little Billy Goat Gruff," he squeaked. "I'm not crossing the bridge!"

Comprehension

1   What does the first sentence tell you about the Three Billy Goats Gruff?

2   Why did Little Billy Goat Gruff suggest they should go across the bridge?

3   What was dangerous about crossing the bridge?

4   Why did Little Billy Goat Gruff cross the bridge first?

5   What happened when Little Billy Goat Gruff crossed the bridge?

6   Who do you think was the greediest billy goat? Why?

7   Who do you think was the most cowardly billy goat? Why?

8   How do you think Little Billy Goat Gruff felt when the troll jumped out?

Spelling

'o-e', 'ow' and 'oa'

Sometimes, different groups of letters can make the same sound. The letters '**o-e**', '**ow**' and '**oa**' sometimes sound the same. For example:

"I h**o**p**e** he won't thr**ow** me in the river," said Little Billy G**oa**t Gruff.

A Choose the correct word to go with each picture.
Write your answers.

1
glow   goat

2
bowl   bone

3
road   rope

4
stone   snow

5
boat   bow

6
soak   smoke

B Copy and complete each word by adding 'o-e', 'ow' or 'oa'.

1 r _ s _   2 fl _ _ t   3 gr _ _

4 sl _ p _   5 m _ _   6 g _ _ l

7 j _ k _   8 r _ _ s t   9 l _ _ _

Writing sentences

Speech marks

When we write the exact words a person said, we put **speech marks** around them. For example:

"Let's go across the bridge to that other field," said Little Billy Goat Gruff.

A In each question, copy the exact words the goat said.
The first one has been done to help you.

1 "There is plenty of good grass there," said Little Billy Goat Gruff.

There is plenty of good grass there.

2 "I don't want to be eaten," said Big Billy Goat Gruff.

3 "We need some more grass to eat," said Middle Billy Goat Gruff.

B Copy each sentence below.
Draw circles around the speech marks and draw a line under the exact words that were said.

Use a ruler when you draw a line under the words.

1 "Little Billy Goat Gruff can go first," said Middle Billy Goat Gruff.

2 "Who is crossing my bridge?" roared the troll.

Writing

Descriptions

You are going to make a poster about each Billy Goat Gruff.
For each poster:

1 Write the name of the goat as a title.

2 Draw a picture of the goat.

3 Write some sentences to describe what he looks like.

4 Use the words from the story to describe his character.

Check-up 2

Spelling

A For each word, write another word that means the **opposite**.

1 come   2 down   3 soft

4 asleep   5 in   6 high

B Add '**un**' or '**dis**' to make the opposite of each word.

1 like   2 do   3 true

4 believe   5 connect   6 kind

C Copy each word from the box and split it into its **syllables**. Write down how many syllables it has.

rubbish	carrot	underneath
football	unhappy	slippery
frozen	overcoat	

D Copy these headings.

'ow' words	'o-e' words	'oa' words

Write each word from the box under the correct heading.

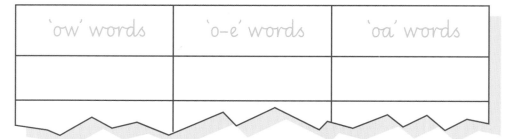

hole	bone	blow	soap	show
snow	road	stone	coal	code

Writing sentences   **A**   Copy these sentences neatly, adding '**was**' or '**were**' in each gap.

The time _____ 8 o'clock. Ben and I _____ ready for school. We _____ surprised to see heavy snow falling outside. I _____ really excited and we _____ both pleased when Mum said Ben and I _____ allowed to stay at home.

B   Draw a picture of your teacher. Add a speech bubble and write what your teacher might be saying.

C   Copy the exact words Ben's mum said.

"Put on your coat before you go into the garden," Mum told Ben.

A Book Cover

The cover of a book can tell us a lot about the book.
This is the front cover of a book.

Mr Timms
Catches a Train

Kim Green

Comprehension

A 1 What is the title of the book?

2 Who is the author?

This is the back cover of the book.

Mr Timms takes a simple trip on a train to visit the dentist. What could go wrong? Well, it all started when Mr Timms got on the wrong train!

What children said about this book:
"Brilliant! The best Mr Timms book I have read."
"The funniest book I've ever read!"

Other Mr Timms books by Kim Green:

Mr Timms Buys a Car
Mr Timms Learns to Fly
Mr Timms Goes on Holiday

Unicorn Books

Comprehension

B 1 What is the name of the publisher?

2 What does the back cover tell you about the story?

3 What did the children who had read the book think about it?

4 What other books has Kim Green written?

5 Do you or don't you like the picture on the cover? Why?

6 Would you like to read the book or not? Why?

Spelling

'oo'

Sometimes, a group of letters can make different sounds.
For example:

I read a **b**oo**k** about **f**oo**d**.

A Copy the headings below.

'oo' sounds like 'oo' in 'book'	'oo' sounds like 'oo' in 'food'

Write each word from the box under the correct heading.

hook	wood	soon	good	roof	moon	hood
spoon	shook	soot	too	wool	hoof	goose
moose	stood	pool	brook	stool	crook	

B Here is a silly sentence using lots of 'oo' words:

The c**oo**k t**oo**k her b**oo**k and threw it in the br**oo**k.

Write your own silly sentence, using as many 'oo' words as
you can.

Writing sentences

Commas in lists

Remember, we put **commas** between the words in a list.
We do not put a comma before the words 'or' or 'and'.

Remember, don't
put a comma
before 'or' or
'and'.

A Copy these sentences, putting in the missing commas
and full stops.

1 I need a book about trains buses bikes cars or lorries

2 We bought apples butter milk bread and eggs

3 I can come to tea on Monday Tuesday Thursday
Saturday or Sunday

Don't forget the commas.

B Write a sentence listing at least four things you don't like to eat.

Start like this:

I don't like to eat _____

Writing

A book cover

Remember, a **book cover** gives us lots of information about the book.

You are going to design a front cover and a back cover for a book. Choose one of these book titles.

• Jo's New Bike

• The Car That Could Talk

• The Ship That Vanished

1 Fold a sheet of paper in half.

2 On the front cover, put:
   • the title
   • the author's name
   • an eye-catching illustration.

3 On the back cover, put:
   • information about the story
   • what people think of the book
   • the name of the publisher
   • titles of other books by the author.

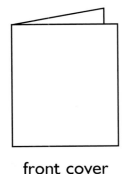

front cover

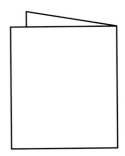

back cover

I Wonder Why Dad is so Thoroughly Mad

I wonder why Dad is so thoroughly mad,
I can't understand it at all,
unless it's the bee still afloat in his tea,
or his underwear, pinned to the wall.

Perhaps it's the dye on his favourite tie,
or the mousetrap that snapped at his shoe,
or the pipeful of gum that he found with his thumb,
or the toilet, sealed tightly with glue.

It can't be the bread crumbled up in his bed,
or the slugs someone left in the hall,
I wonder why Dad is so thoroughly mad,
I can't understand it at all.

Comprehension

1   Look at the first verse.
    What two things have happened that could have made Dad 'mad'?

2   Look at the second verse.
    Which of the four things do you think would make Dad most 'mad'? Why?

3   Look at the third verse.
    What two things have happened that could have made Dad 'mad'?

4   If you were Dad, what would have made you the most 'mad'? Why?

5   Do you or don't you find this poem funny? Why?

Spelling

'ful' and 'ly'

Sometimes, a group of letters is added to the end of a word. This is called a **suffix**. For example:

thorough + 'ly' = thoroughly   pipe + 'ful' = pipeful

'ly' and 'ful' are suffixes.

A 1 Add the suffix 'ly' to each word.
The first one has been done to help you.

a quiet   quietly

b bad   c safe   d kind

e quick   f surprising   g neat

2 Write a sentence that includes one of the 'ly' words you made in question 1.

Notice that the suffix 'ful' has only one 'l'.

B 1 Add the suffix 'ful' to each word.
The first one has been done to help you.

a help   helpful

b pain   c hope   d spite

e use   f wonder   g thought

2 Write a sentence that includes one of the 'ful' words you made in question 1.

Writing sentences

Male and female words

'Male' and 'female' words are called **gender words**.

Some words are always used for boys, men and male animals. For example:

he   him   his

Some words are always used for girls, women and female animals. For example:

she   her   hers

Some words can be used for either males or females. For example:

I   we   us   they   it

A Copy the sentences below but, in place of the yellow words, use one of the small words from the box.
The first one has been done to help you.

He ✓	We	her	They	she ✓
hers	him	She	we	it

1 Dad **said** Sara **should help**.

   He said she should help.

2 Jess and I **said we would help** Dad.

3 Gran **said** the cup of tea **was** Gran's cup of tea.

4 My friends **said** my sister and I **should help**
   my mum.

B Write a sentence about the poem on page 36. Include the words 'he' and 'his'.

Writing

Funny poems

> Poetry can often be **funny** when it is written about people who act in a silly way or have silly things happen to them.

You are going to write a poem called 'I Wonder Why Mum is so Thoroughly Glum'.
Follow the pattern of the poem on page 36.

Begin your poem:

I wonder why Mum is so thoroughly glum,

I can't understand it at all,

third line:
A word somewhere in the middle of this line should rhyme with the word at the end of the line, like:
'unless it's the **bee** still afloat in his **tea**'.

fourth line:
The word at the end of this line should rhyme with 'all', like:
'or his underwear, pinned to the **wall**.'

One Snowy Night

One winter's night it was so cold it began to snow. Great big snowflakes fell past the window of Percy's hut.

"Brrr," said Percy. "I think I'll need an extra blanket tonight."

He made himself some hot cocoa and got ready for bed.

Suddenly, Percy heard a tapping sound. There was somebody at the door.

"Now who can that be at this time of night?" thought Percy. He went to the door and looked out.

There on the step was a squirrel. It looked very cold
and miserable.

"I can't get to sleep, Percy," said the squirrel.
"My bed is full of snow."

"Oh dear," said Percy. "Never mind, I've got plenty
of room for two."

The squirrel snuggled down next to Percy and soon
began to feel warm.

Knock! Knock!
It was the door again.

"Now who can
that be?" thought Percy.

Standing outside were two shivering rabbits.

"It's f-freezing," said one rabbit.

"We're f-frozen," said the other.

"You poor things," said Percy. "Come in and warm up."

The rabbits squeezed into the bed next to Percy and the squirrel. There wasn't much room.

"Could you face the other way?" Percy asked the squirrel. "Your tail is tickling my nose."

Knock! Knock!

"Oh dear," said Percy. "Now there's someone else at the door!"

Comprehension

1   Where does the story take place?

2   What is the weather like in the story?

3   Who was the first to knock at Percy's door? Why?

4   Who knocked at Percy's door after that? Why?

5   When there was a third knock at the door, Percy said, "Now there's someone else at the door!" Who do you think might be at the door?

6   What kind of person do you think Percy is? Why?

Spelling

'wh' words

Words that start a question often begin with '**wh**'. For example:

what   where   when   who   why   which

Notice that you can't hear the 'h' in 'wh' when you say these question words.

A Copy the sentences below, filling in the missing 'wh' words and add the missing question marks.

1 _____ is your favourite type of weather __

2 _____ do you like that type of weather __

3 _____ do you like to go when the weather is like that __

4 _____ do you like to play with __

5 _____ is the weather hot and sunny __

6 _____ do you prefer, sunshine or snow __

B Now write a sentence to answer each question in part A. Make sure each sentence begins with a capital letter and ends with a full stop.

Writing sentences

Making questions

We can often make a sentence into a **question** by moving some words and changing some words. For example:

Sentence:	Percy made himself some hot cocoa.
Question:	What did Percy make himself?

Don't forget the question marks.

A Write a question to match each answer.

1 The story took place in Percy's hut.

2 Percy put an extra blanket on his bed.

3 A squirrel was waiting outside the door.

4 The rabbits were shivering with cold.

B 1 Write your own question about:
   a the story
   b Percy.

2 Write a sentence to answer each question.

Writing

Setting, plot and characters

When you write a story you need to think about:

the setting   <u>where</u> and <u>when</u> your story happens

the plot   <u>what</u> happens in your story

the characters   <u>who</u> is in your story.

You are going to plan a story called 'One Windy Night'.

1   Write the title 'One Windy Night' at the top of a piece of paper.

2   Draw three columns on the paper and write these headings.

Setting	Plot	Characters

3   Think about where and when your story happens.
In the first column, write some words to describe where and when.

4   Think about what happens in the story.
In the second column, write notes about what happens.

5   Think about the characters in your story.
In the third column, write their names, what they look like and what type of characters they are.

Check-up 3

A Write an '**ou**' or '**ow**' word to go with each picture.

1
2
3

B Write an '**ai**', '**ay**' or '**a-e**' word to go with each picture.

1
2
3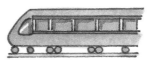
4

C For each word, write a word that means the **opposite**.

1 in   2 yes   3 clean   4 wet   5 new

D Make the opposite of each word by adding '**un**' or '**dis**' at the beginning.

1 wanted   2 like   3 certain   4 obey

E Add '**ing**' and then '**ed**' to each word.

1 clean   2 wait   3 play   4 watch

F Copy each word, and draw a line to divide it into its **syllables**.

1 party   2 enjoyment   3 hopefully

4 smiling   5 happy   6 eating

G For each word below, write three words that rhyme and have the same letter pattern.

1 boat   2 throw   3 rose

4 food   5 cook   6 moon

H Add ' **ly** ' or ' **ful** ' to each word.

1 quiet   2 smart   3 care

4 help   5 wonder   6 hope

I Write four question words that begin with ' **wh** '.

Writing sentences

A Write each letter as a **capital letter**.

1 k   2 f   3 w   4 m

5 e   6 q   7 r   8 y

B Copy and complete these sentences, using people's names.

1   My name is _____.

2   I live with _____.

C Copy these sentences, putting in the missing **capital letters**, **full stops** and **question marks**.

1   i have a pet dog

2   his name is dexter

3   do you have a pet

4   what is its name

D Copy these sentences, adding 'was' or 'were' in each gap.

1 Simon _____ sorry when his friend Josh moved to a new town.

2 They _____ always playing together.

3 Josh _____ Simon's best friend.

E Draw a picture of Simon waving goodbye to Josh.
Add a speech bubble and write what you think Simon is saying.

F Write the words Josh actually said.

"I will write to you and come to visit you soon,"
Josh called as the car pulled away.

G Copy this sentence, adding the missing **capital letter**, **commas** and **full stop**.

at the wildlife park we saw zebras monkeys giraffes wolves penguins snakes and an elephant

H Write down a **question** for which this sentence could be the answer:

I live on the fifth floor of a block of flats in Nuffield Road.